Celebrations in My World

Thanksgiving

Lynn Peppas

Crabtree Publishing Company

www.crabtreebooks.com

Crabtree Publishing Company

www.crabtreebooks.com

Author: Lynn Peppas
Coordinating editor: Chester Fisher
Series and project editor: Penny Dowdy
Editor: Adrianna Morganelli
Proofreader: Crystal Sikkens
Project editor: Robert Walker
Production coordinator: Katherine Berti
Prepress technician: Katherine Berti
Project manager: Kumar Kunal (Q2AMEDIA)
Art direction: Dibakar Acharjee (Q2AMEDIA)
Cover design: Tarang Saggar (Q2AMEDIA)
Design: Ritu Chopra (Q2AMEDIA)
Photo research: Farheen Aadil (Q2AMEDIA)

Photographs:
123rf: Talyaona: p. 10; Cathy Yeulet: p. 17
Alamy: Michael Grant: p. 8; John Terence Turner: p. 18;
    Visions Of America, LLC: p. 23; Jim West: p. 28
BigStockPhoto: Gina Smith: p. 6
The Bridgeman Art Library: Dreweatt Neate Fine Art Auctioneers,
    Newbury, Berks, UK: p. 9
Corbis: Bettmann: p. 7, 11–12, 19; Jose Luis Pelaez, Inc.: p. 27;
    Ariel Skelley: p. 1, 24; Larry Williams: p. 26
Corbis Sygma: Ciniglio Lorenzo: p. 22
Dreamstime: Lucretia: p. 4
Getty Images: Archive Photos/Stringer: p. 13; Harry How/Staff: p. 31;
    A. Messerschmidt/Staff: p. 25; Alex Wong/Staff: p. 15
iStockphoto.com: front cover
Jupiter Images: p. 30; Comstock Images: p. 29
PhotoDisc, Market Fresh: folio glyph
Shutterstock: Avava: p. 16; Joy Brown: p. 14; Jan Bruder: p. 21;
    Tatiana Grozetskaya: p. 5; Laura Stone: p. 20

Library and Archives Canada Cataloguing in Publication

Peppas, Lynn
        Thanksgiving / Lynn Peppas.

(Celebrations in my world)
Includes index.
ISBN 978-0-7787-4291-3 (bound).--ISBN 978-0-7787-4309-5 (pbk.)

        1. Thanksgiving Day--Juvenile literature.
I. Title. II. Series: Celebrations in my world

GT4975.P46 2009   j394.2649   C2009-900234-5

Library of Congress Cataloging-in-Publication Data

Peppas, Lynn.
    Thanksgiving / Lynn Peppas.
        p. cm. -- (Celebrations in my world)
    Includes index.
    ISBN 978-0-7787-4309-5 (pbk. : alk. paper) -- ISBN 978-0-7787-4291-3
(reinforced library binding : alk. paper)
    1. Thanksgiving Day--Juvenile literature. I. Title. II. Series.

    GT4975.P47 2009
    394.2649--dc22

                                                2009000326

Crabtree Publishing Company

www.crabtreebooks.com   1-800-387-7650

Published in Canada
Crabtree Publishing
616 Welland Ave.
St. Catharines, ON
L2M 5V6

Published in the United States
Crabtree Publishing
PMB16A
350 Fifth Ave., Suite 3308
New York, NY 10118

Published in the United Kingdom
Crabtree Publishing
White Cross Mills
High Town, Lancaster
LA1 4XS

Published in Australia
Crabtree Publishing
386 Mt. Alexander Rd.
Ascot Vale (Melbourne)
VIC 3032

Contents

What is Thanksgiving?

Thanksgiving Day is a **harvest** holiday. On this day, Americans and Canadians give thanks for the food and **blessings** they have been given.

Thanksgiving Day is in autumn. In autumn, farmers harvest, or gather, their crops.

● These farmers are harvesting their crops in autumn.

DID YOU KNOW?

In the United States, the day after Thanksgiving is one of the busiest shopping days of the year. People start to shop for Christmas.

Farmers grow enough food to last them during the cold, winter months. Thanksgiving is a time to give thanks for good harvests.

Thanksgiving Day is always in autumn, when the leaves change colors.

A National Holiday

Thanksgiving Day is a **national** holiday. For many, it is a day off from school or work. Banks, post offices, schools, and many businesses close for the day.

In America, President George Washington made Thursday, November 26, 1789, a Thanksgiving holiday. It was not celebrated again the next year.

● Businesses close on Thanksgiving Day so that families can spend time together.

DID YOU KNOW?

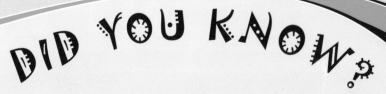

*President Abraham Lincoln made Thanksgiving Day a national holiday to help bring Americans together during a **civil war**.*

In 1939, President Roosevelt officially made Thanksgiving the fourth Thursday of November.

In 1863, President Abraham Lincoln declared Thanksgiving Day an **annual** holiday. People would celebrate Thanksgiving on the last Thursday of November. In 1939, President Franklin D. Roosevelt changed it to the fourth Thursday in November.

7

Past Celebrations

People gave thanks for good harvests long before the North American Thanksgiving. Thousands of years ago, people believed that gods controlled the seasons. To thank their gods, people held special harvest festivals.

- The ancient Greeks believed the goddess Demeter controlled crops.

DID YOU KNOW?

In ancient Greece, people held festivals every year to honor their goddess of crops, Demeter.

Hundreds of years ago, people held a harvest festival called Michaelmas. They celebrated by having a feast. This **tradition** of celebrating harvests with feasts still happens today. In North America, we call it Thanksgiving Day.

Michaelmas was a harvest festival long before the first Thanksgiving.

The Pilgrims

In 1620, almost 100 **Pilgrims** left England and founded the **colony** of Plymouth in New England. Some left because the king would not let them worship the way they wanted.

Pilgrims found a cold wilderness with no roads or cities.

DID YOU KNOW?

The Pilgrims had no homes and little food during their first winter. Many became sick, and almost half of them died.

The leaders in England forced others to leave. They sailed on a ship called the *Mayflower*. The Pilgrims landed in Plymouth, Massachusetts in December, 1620.

Pilgrims traveled for months on the ship called the *Mayflower*.

11

The First Thanksgiving

The Pilgrims needed to plant crops in the spring of 1621. The crops would feed their families in their new colony. Native Americans, called the Wampanoag, lived in this area long before the Pilgrims arrived.

Pilgrims thanked God for their harvest by having a feast in 1621.

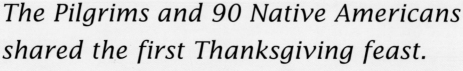

DID YOU KNOW?

The Pilgrims and 90 Native Americans shared the first Thanksgiving feast.

Native Americans taught the Pilgrims what crops to grow.

The Wampanoag taught the Pilgrims what crops to grow. Pilgrims wanted to give thanks for their harvest. They invited the Native Americans to their feast.

Turkeys!

Pilgrims may have enjoyed wild turkey for their first Thanksgiving. No one knows for sure. Today, eating turkey on this holiday is very popular. Many people in the United States call Thanksgiving Day "Turkey Day."

Farmers raise turkeys on farms. A large group of turkeys is called a flock.

DID YOU KNOW?

In the United States, turkey farmers raise over 46 million turkeys for Thanksgiving dinners.

President Abraham Lincoln was the first American president to **pardon** a Thanksgiving Day turkey. This pardon meant that the turkey would not be cooked for the president's Thanksgiving dinner. The president's pardon became a yearly tradition in 1947.

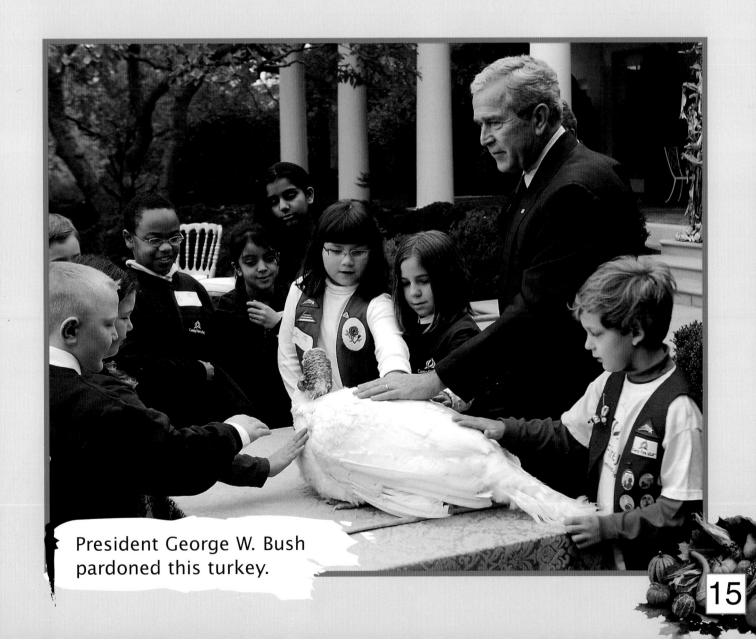

President George W. Bush pardoned this turkey.

Thanksgiving Dinner

People celebrate Thanksgiving Day by sharing a big dinner. Traditional Thanksgiving dinners include turkey served with cranberry sauce and sweet potatoes. Most families enjoy pumpkin pie for dessert.

• Preparing a feast is a tradition for Thanksgiving Day.

DID YOU KNOW?

Most cooks fill their turkeys with bread, rice, or nuts. Some people call this "stuffing." Others call it "dressing."

Today's Thanksgiving dinners include some of the same foods the Pilgrims ate at their feast. Native Americans taught the Pilgrims to grow corn, beans, and pumpkins. These foods helped the Pilgrims survive. We still enjoy them today!

Families and friends gather together for a traditional Thanksgiving turkey dinner.

Thanksgiving Songs

On Thanksgiving Day, people like to sing traditional songs and **hymns**. One popular hymn is "Come, Ye Thankful People, Come." It was written almost 200 years ago.

People like to sing Thanksgiving songs and hymns.

DID YOU KNOW?

Lydia Maria Child was born in Massachusetts in 1802. Some of her writings tell about the unfair treatment of Native Americans.

Lydia Maria Child wrote about traveling to her grandparents' home for Thanksgiving dinner.

American Lydia Maria Child wrote the famous Thanksgiving song, "Over the River and Through the Woods" in 1844. This song shares her memories of traveling to her grandparents' home for Thanksgiving dinner.

19

Thanksgiving Symbols

The cornucopia is a popular Thanksgiving **symbol**. It is sometimes called a horn of plenty. It is a horn or a basket shaped like a horn overflowing with food.

A cornucopia is shaped like a horn. It is sometimes called a horn of plenty.

DID YOU KNOW?

Maize, or Indian corn, is a colorful corn often used for decorating during Thanksgiving.

For Thanksgiving, people decorate with pumpkins and corn. Remember that Native Americans taught the Pilgrims to grow these foods.

Maize, or Indian corn, is a popular Thanksgiving decoration.

Thanksgiving Parades

Many cities have Thanksgiving Day parades. The parades have floats, clowns, marching bands, and even Santa Claus.

Some people ride on floats in the Thanksgiving Day Parade.

DID YOU KNOW?

American department store Macy's started the tradition of having huge helium balloons shaped like cartoon characters in their parades.

Some balloons in the Macy's Thanksgiving parade stand over 60 feet (18 meters) tall!

New York City has the Macy's Thanksgiving Day Parade. On Thanksgiving morning, thousands of people stand on the streets to watch the parade. Millions more watch on television.

Thanksgiving Sports

Families often play or watch sports on television on Thanksgiving Day. Football is the holiday's most popular sport.

Family and friends get together on Thanksgiving Day to play football.

DID YOU KNOW?

The Detroit Lions started the NFL tradition of the annual Thanksgiving Day football game in 1934.

The American football tradition began in the 1800s. Many football teams still play games on Thanksgiving Day. The National Football League's competition is called the Thanksgiving Day Classic.

Every year on Thanksgiving, the NFL holds their Thanksgiving Day Classic.

Giving Thanks

Gathering to watch parades and sports is fun. A turkey dinner is delicious. However, the true reason for the holiday is to give thanks for the good things in our lives.

This family gives thanks before eating their turkey dinner.

DID YOU KNOW?

Some families say a special prayer before eating their turkey dinners. They give thanks for their many blessings.

People give thanks for plentiful food and good health. Other people are thankful for spending time with people they love. In some families, each person says what they are thankful for.

Children enjoy making Thanksgiving Day crafts.

Giving to Others

People help the poor or homeless at Thanksgiving. Some **donate** food or money to people in need. Others **volunteer** their time to work at charities.

Soup kitchens prepare Thanksgiving dinners for people who do not have food.

DID YOU KNOW?

A *food drive* is an organized collection of food. After the food is collected, it is brought to a food bank where it is sorted and then given to the poor.

People help cook and serve turkey dinners at local soup kitchens. They also help clean up afterward.

Thanksgiving is a time of being with people. Many visit relatives or friends who cannot get out to visit them.

Thanksgiving is a time to get together with the people you love.

Thanksgiving in Canada

Thanksgiving in Canada became popular in the 1800s. Thanksgiving Day did not become a national Canadian holiday until 1957.

● Canadians celebrate their Thanksgiving Day in October.

DID YOU KNOW?

In Canada, the harvest season is earlier than in the United States.

Canadian Thanksgivings are similar to the U.S. holiday. People gather to share a meal and give thanks for plentiful harvests. Just like their neighbors, the Canadian Football League (CFL) holds a Thanksgiving Day Classic on their Thanksgiving Day.

- Football is also a big part of the Thanksgiving Day festivities in Canada.

Glossary

annual Occurring every year at the same time

blessings Good things in a person's life

civil war A war between people living in the same country

colony An area where people live in a new country

donate To give to someone in need

food drive Food items collected by a group of people for the needy

harvest The season when farmers gather crops

hymn A religious song

national Belonging to one country or nation

pardon To give a person or animal freedom

Pilgrims English settlers who founded the colony of Plymouth

symbol An object that stands for something else

tradition A custom handed down from one generation to another

volunteer Work without payment

Index

Printed in the U.S.A.—CG